CRANES

Lynn Peppas
Crabtree Publishing Company
www.crabtreebooks.com

Created by Bobbie Kalman

Author
Lynn Peppas

**Publishing plan research
and development**
Sean Charlebois, Reagan Miller
Crabtree Publishing Company

Editorial director
Kathy Middleton

Editor
Molly Aloian

Proofreader
Crystal Sikkens

Photo research
Samara Parent

Design
Samara Parent

**Production coordinator
and prepress technician**
Samara Parent

Print coordinator
Katherine Berti

Photographs
Dreamstime.com: back cover, pages 16, 17, 26-27
Shutterstock.com: front cover, title page, pages 3, 4, 5 (both),
    6-7, 8, 9, 10, 11, 14-15, 18, 20, 21, 22, 23, 24, 25, 29 (both);
    Bruce Leibowitz: page 29 (top); Gila Photography: page
    29 (bottom)
Thinkstock.com: pages 12, 13, 14 (bottom)
Wikimedia Commons: ©Louise Docker: page 19;
    ©Tu7uh: page 28, ©Haakman: pages 30-31

Library and Archives Canada Cataloguing in Publication

Peppas, Lynn
    Cranes / Lynn Peppas.

(Vehicles on the move)
Includes index.
Issued also in electronic format.
ISBN 978-0-7787-3018-7 (bound).--ISBN 978-0-7787-3023-1 (pbk.)

    1. Cranes, derricks, etc.--Juvenile literature. I. Title. II. Series:
Vehicles on the move

TJ1363.P47 2012   j621.8'73   C2012-900890-7

Library of Congress Cataloging-in-Publication Data

Peppas, Lynn.
    Cranes / Lynn Peppas.
        p. cm. -- (Vehicles on the move)
    Includes index.
    Audience: Grades K-3.
    ISBN 978-0-7787-3018-7 (library binding : alk. paper) --
    ISBN 978-0-7787-3023-1 (pbk. : alk. paper) -- ISBN 978-1-4271-7942-5
    (electronic pdf) -- ISBN 978-1-4271-8057-5 (electronic html)
    1. Cranes--Juvenile literature. I. Title.

    TJ1363.P375 2012
    621.8'73--dc23
                                                          2012004059

Crabtree Publishing Company

www.crabtreebooks.com   1-800-387-7650

Printed in Canada/042012/KR20120316

Published in Canada
Crabtree Publishing
616 Welland Ave.
St. Catharines, Ontario
L2M 5V6

Published in the United States
Crabtree Publishing
PMB 59051
350 Fifth Avenue, 59th Floor
New York, New York 10118

Published in the United Kingdom
Crabtree Publishing
Maritime House
Basin Road North, Hove
BN41 1WR

Published in Australia
Crabtree Publishing
3 Charles Street
Coburg North
VIC 3058

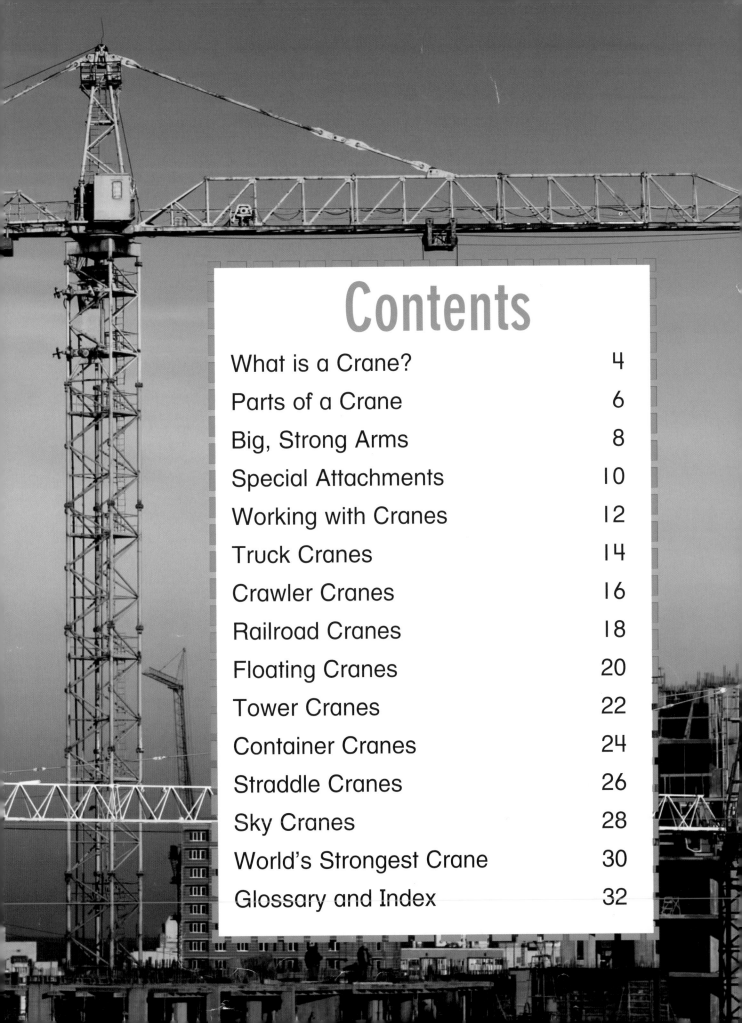

Contents

What is a Crane?

A crane is a vehicle. A vehicle is a machine that moves and does work. A crane picks heavy objects up from one place and moves them to another. It can lift loads that no other vehicle can. A crane has to be powerful to lift and move such heavy things!

*Some cranes have arms that swivel, or turn in a circle, on **turntables**. This helps them move a load from one place to another.*

Cranes do many different kinds of jobs. They come in different shapes and sizes. Some cranes can drive. Others must stay in one place at all times.

A crane is also a type of bird. A crane has a long neck and long legs. The vehicles look a lot like the birds!

Parts of a Crane

The parts of a crane help it lift and move large loads. All parts work together to do the job safely. The main parts of a crane are the tower, the pulley, cables, a hook, a cab, and the arm, which is also called the jib or boom.

cab

tower

jib

cable

A crane lifts objects using a simple machine called a pulley. A pulley is a steel wheel with a **groove** in the middle. Steel cables fit into the pulley. A motor pulls in the cable to lift heavy loads up. It lets out cable to put the load down.

pully

hook

Big, Strong Arms

trolley

The arms of a crane lift and carry heavy loads. Different crane arms do different kinds of jobs. A jib is a long arm that reaches out from the tower. Tall Tower cranes have jibs. Tower cranes have a trolley that hangs from the bottom of the jib. It moves from one end of the jib to the other on wheels.

When the trolley is close to the tower, the tower crane can carry heavier loads. The farther away from the tower the trolley moves, the less the crane can carry.

Some cranes have telescopic booms. Telescopic means the arm, or boom, has more sections that fit inside it. When the crane must reach farther up, these sections come out to make the boom longer and reach higher.

jib

Some telescopic booms also have a jib attached to the end of the boom. When all the telescopic sections are extended, the jib can be extended to make the crane even higher.

Special Attachments

Heavy loads come in all shapes and sizes. Cranes need special attachments to lift different kinds of loads. An attachment is something that is put on a machine to help it do a special kind of job.

Spreaders are attachments that clamp onto large containers.

Some cranes move objects using large hooks that are attached to a pulley that holds the cable. Other cranes have buckets for digging dirt or **forklifts** for stacking boxes.

Some cranes have powerful magnets that lift metal objects.

Working With Cranes

A person who works a crane is called a crane **operator**. The crane operator sits in the crane's cab. The cab is a small area with **controls** that move the crane. The crane operator uses pedals and levers to make the crane do work.

A crane operator has to go through special training and tests to learn how to use all the controls before operating a crane.

Some cranes, such as truck cranes, have cabs that are near the ground. Other cabs, such as the cabs on tower cranes, are high up in the air. These crane operators must climb tall ladders to get to the cab.

Cabs have large windows so crane operators can see clearly all around.

Truck Cranes

A truck crane can drive on most roads or highways to move from job to job. The truck part is called the lower. The crane part is called the upper. Most truck cranes have one engine that drives the vehicle and operates the crane.

Truck cranes have a telescopic boom that can be lengthened for use on a jobsite, and shortened when traveling to the next job.

Truck cranes use **outriggers** when they are lifting and moving heavy objects. Outriggers are steel feet that come out from the sides of the truck. They help balance the truck so it will not roll over when working.

outriggers

15

Crawler Cranes

A crawler crane moves on a set of tracks. Tracks make it very sturdy. Tracks are made of steel plates that are **linked**, or joined, together. Crawler cranes travel over loose, crumbly, or wet ground without sinking or sliding. They move slowly over short distances carrying heavy weights.

A crawler crane's tracks are sometimes called caterpillar tracks.

Crawler cranes are very big and heavy. The largest crawler cranes can lift up to 3,000 tons (2,722 metric tons). To move from one jobsite to another, these cranes must be taken apart. The parts are loaded onto transport trucks, trains, or ships to be taken to the next job.

Crawler cranes do not need outriggers because their tracks keep them sturdy.

Railroad Cranes

A railroad crane moves on railroad lines. The crane sits on a flat railroad car on tracks. Railroad cranes load and unload **cargo** on and off of trains. Railroad cranes are also used to carry and lay new railroad tracks on the ground.

This railroad crane is unloading loose stone from a railroad car.

Wrecking cranes are used when trains have accidents. These large railroad cranes can travel on the tracks to the accident site. They can lift railroad cars and locomotives back onto the track. A locomotive is a railway vehicle that moves the train.

This locomotive is getting lifted back onto the tracks by a wrecking crane after an accident.

Floating Cranes

Floating cranes are just what they sound like. They are cranes that float on water! Another name for floating cranes is sheerlegs. Floating cranes are used for jobs such as building ships and loading or unloading cargo from ships. Some lift up ships that have sunk underwater.

The largest floating crane in the world is from Japan and is named Kaisho. It can lift over 4,000 tons (3,628 metric tons).

A floating crane is attached to a barge. A barge is a low, flat-bottomed boat. Some floating cranes have their own engines and can move on their own. Other floating cranes must be pulled by tugboats.

Tower Cranes

A tower crane is one of the tallest vehicles in the world. They are fixed cranes that cannot move to different places on their own. Tower cranes are brought in pieces by a truck and then put together at the jobsite. When the job is done, they are taken apart and moved to another jobsite.

Tower cranes are used to help build tall buildings. After a building is done, a smaller crane is usually attached to the top of the building to help take the tower crane apart.

Tower cranes often work at construction sites. They are built and attached to a large, concrete bottom. They can swing around in a full circle. They lift heavy objects up to 20 tons (18 metric tons). They can reach heights of 265 feet (81 meters). That's higher than a 20-story building!

Tower cranes can be built as tall as they need to be to get the job done.

Container Cranes

A container crane is a large, fixed crane that cannot move to different places. Container cranes move containers to and from ships at shipping docks. A dock is a platform that ships park alongside while their cargo gets loaded and unloaded.

Most container cranes lift one container at a time. However, some newer cranes can lift up to four containers at once.

Container cranes use a spreader attachment that is connected to the trolley of the crane. The spreader attaches to a container and lifts the container using a pulley. The trolley then moves along the arm of the crane carrying the container to where it needs to go.

Straddle Cranes

A straddle crane stands overtop of heavy loads. Straddle means to stand with legs spread far apart. Straddle cranes have two legs on either side. The overhead bar that runs between the two legs is called the bridge.

Straddle cranes have overhead **hoists** that lift heavy objects. Some straddle cranes can move on wheels or rails. Others are fixed to the ground. Straddle cranes are used to lift very heavy loads.

Straddle cranes are sometimes called bridge or gantry cranes.

legs

bridge

hoist

legs

Sky Cranes

Helicopters made to lift and carry heavy loads are called sky cranes. A helicopter is a vehicle that can fly and **hover**. They fly to places that other vehicles cannot get to.

This sky crane is putting up a tall pole that will have an antenna on top.

right: Sky cranes can carry 2,650 gallons (10,031 liters) in each load.

bottom: Sky cranes suck water up into large tanks with a hose.

Sky cranes lift loads to the tops of buildings and shopping centers. They lift large, freshly cut trees from forests where large trucks cannot go. They also help fight forest fires. They carry large water tanks and drop water over wildfires that fire trucks cannot get to.

World's Strongest Crane

The strongest crane in the world is a straddle or bridge crane found in Yantai, China. It is called Taisun. It holds the world's record for most weight lifted. The Taisun can lift over 22,000 tons (20,000 metric tons).

The Taisun is used to build offshore drilling rigs. Offshore drilling rigs drill for oil in Earth's oceans. The Taisun stands over 370 feet (113 meters) tall. That is about the height of a 30-story building!

The red and white Taisun crane is shown here building a floating drilling rig.

Glossary

cargo Goods or products that are packaged together to be carried on trains, trucks, aircraft, or ships

controls A set of devices that allow a person to work the moving parts of a machine

forklift A machine that uses steel fingers to lift objects

groove A long, narrow indent

hoist A machine that lifts or lowers objects with a steel cable around a wheel

hover The ability to hang in one place in the air for a long time

link One part that is attached to other pieces to make a whole, such as a chain

operator A person who can do work using a machine

outriggers An added part that extends from the main part to give support

turntable A platform or table that can turn around

Index